MY LITTLE
Gratitude
JOURNAL

THIS BOOK BELONGS TO:

_____

PAIGE YELLE IS A CHRISTIAN WIFE, MOM, SMALL BUSINESS OWNER, AND ADOPTION ADVOCATE. SHE RECENTLY WENT SKYDIVING, ROCKY MOUNTAIN CLIMBING, AND RODE A MECHANICAL BULL SHE NAMED FU MANCHU. HER SOUTHERN ACCENT COMES IN STRONG ANYTIME SHE'S ASKED ABOUT SEC FOOTBALL, ALTHOUGH SHE'S BEEN TRANSPLANTED TO OKLAHOMA. SHE REMAINS THANKFUL FOR THE LITTLE THINGS IN LIFE LIKE: FRESH BISCUITS AND FIG PRESERVES, JUMPING ON THE TRAMPOLINE WITH HER GIRLS, SINGING OFF KEY IN THE CAR, AND SILLY DANCING ANY CHANCE SHE GETS.

STAY IN TOUCH!
INSTAGRAM: @PAIGEYELLE

MY LITTLE GRATITUDE JOURNAL

COPYRIGHT 2015. ALL RIGHTS RESERVED.
NO PART OF THIS PUBLICATION MAY BE REPRODUCED, OR STORED IN A RETRIEVAL SYSTEM, OR TRANSMITTED BY ANY FORM OR BY ANY MEANS, ELECTRONIC, MECHANICAL, PHOTOCOPYING, RECORDING, OR OTHERWISE, WITHOUT WRITTEN PERMISSION, EXCEPT IN CONTEXT OF REVIEWS.

WRITTEN BY PAIGE YELLE

MY LITTLE *Gratitude* JOURNAL

YOU MAY HAVE NOTICED THAT THIS IS NOT AN ORDINARY JOURNAL. OF COURSE, IT'S FOR RECORDING, READING, AND SHARING YOUR GRATITUDE MOMENTS, BUT IT'S SO MUCH MORE! IT'S A PATH TO JOY AND FREEDOM FROM SCREEN TIME.

IF YOU'VE FORGOTTEN HOW TO EXPRESS YOURSELF IN MORE THAN 120 CHARACTERS, THEN THIS LITTLE BOOK IS FOR YOU.

YOU'LL FIND COLORING PAGES, SIMPLE QUESTIONNAIRES, DOODLING PROMPTS FOR YOUR IMAGINATION TO RUN FREE, INSPIRATIONAL QUOTES, AND PLACES TO LIST YOUR GRATEFUL MOMENTS.

IT'S SOMETHING TO DO WHEN YOU PUT YOUR PHONE DOWN.

I LOVE A PRETTY JOURNAL, ALTHOUGH PREVIOUSLY WHILE USING A DATED JOURNAL, I WOULD USUALLY STICK WITH IT ABOUT 35 DAYS, AND THEN I'D FIND MYSELF NOT PICKING IT UP FOR 2 WEEKS. UPON THIS REALIZATION I'D EITHER HAVE TO CATCH UP, OR WAIT 347 MORE DAYS TO GET BACK ON SCHEDULE. NOT HAPPENING!

NEVER FEEL LIKE YOU MISSED A DAY TO JOURNAL.

START ANYTIME OF THE YEAR AND NEVER FEEL GUILT AGAIN. THINK OF IT AS A DO-OVER IF YOU MISS DAYS.

WITH ALL THE ACTIVITIES IN THE BOOK, YOU CAN FIND SOMETHING ELSE TO DO WHEN WAITING IN THE CAR LINE. INSTEAD OF CHECKING IN ON SOCIAL MEDIA, YOU CAN **GET BACK YOUR LIFE, REDISCOVER YOUR INTERESTS, AND LIVE IN THE MOMENT!**

TURN THE PAGE AND GET STARTED NOW. SEE HOW YOUR JOY CAN INCREASE BY SIMPLY PUTTING YOUR PHONE DOWN AND WRITING DOWN A SIMPLE MOMENT OF GRATITUDE IN THE MONTHS FOLLOWING. I HOPE YOU ENJOY THIS LITTLE BOOK AS MUCH AS I HAVE!

XOXO,
PAIGE YELLE

#MYLITTLEGRATITUDEJOURNAL

GETTING TO KNOW *me*!

THINGS I LIKE AT THIS STAGE OF MY LIFE:

- 1 _____
_____
_____
_____
_____

- 2 _____
_____
_____
_____
_____

- 3 _____
_____
_____
_____
_____

NO STRESSES HERE! YOU'LL HAVE 2 MORE OPPORTUNITIES TO UPDATE YOUR "LIKES". YOU ARE FREE TO DISCOVER YOURSELF AND CHANGE ANSWERS.

TO HELP GET YOU STARTED, HERE'S MINE: 1) ICE CREAM 2) TICKLING MY PUPPY DOG 3) CATCHING AIR IN A FAST CAR.

(WRITE MONTH HERE)

(WRITE MONTH HERE)

(WRITE MONTH HERE)

Great work!

LIST YOUR TOP 3 *Gratitude* MOMENTS FOR THE LAST MONTH

1.

2.

3.

"YOU WOULDN'T *worry* SO MUCH ABOUT WHAT OTHERS THINK OF YOU IF YOU *realized* HOW SELDOM THEY DO."

— ELEANOR ROOSEVELT

(WRITE MONTH HERE)

(WRITE MONTH HERE)

(WRITE MONTH HERE)

Way to go!

LIST YOUR TOP 3 *Gratitude* MOMENTS FOR THE LAST MONTH

1.

2.

3.

THE SIMPLE ACT OF SAYING *thank you* IS A DEMONSTRATION OF *gratitude* IN RESPONSE TO AN EXPERIENCE THAT WAS MEANINGFUL TO A CUSTOMER OR CITIZEN.

—SIMON MAINWARING

(WRITE MONTH HERE)

(WRITE MONTH HERE)

(WRITE MONTH HERE)

LIST YOUR TOP 3 *Gratitude* MOMENTS FOR THE LAST MONTH

1.

2.

3.

LETTER TO MY 15 YEAR OLD SELF.

"Be who you are and say what you feel because those who mind don't matter and those who matter don't mind."

—DR. SEUSS

YOU'VE NOW REACHED A MILESTONE!
YOU ARE 3 MONTHS INTO THIS *gratitude* JOURNEY

RECORD YOUR TOP 3 GRATITUDE MOMENTS FROM THE LAST 3 MONTHS.
(THAT'S ONE FOR EACH MONTH)
YOU CAN DO IT!

1.

2.

3.

HOW TO DRAW A
puppy

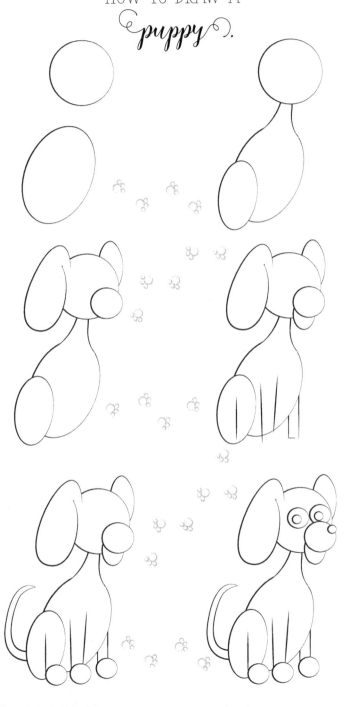

NOW YOU TRY!

(WRITE MONTH HERE)

(WRITE MONTH HERE)

(WRITE MONTH HERE)

LIST YOUR TOP 3 *Gratitude* MOMENTS FOR THE LAST MONTH

- 1
- 2
- 3

You've gotta *dance* like there's nobody watching, *love* like you'll never be hurt, *sing* like there's nobody listening, and live like it's *heaven* on earth.

—William W. Purkey

(WRITE MONTH HERE)

(WRITE MONTH HERE)

(WRITE MONTH HERE)

LIST YOUR TOP 3 *Gratitude* MOMENTS FOR THE LAST MONTH

- 1

- 2

- 3

"There are only two ways to live your *life*. One is as though nothing is a *miracle*. The other is as though everything is a *miracle*."

—Albert Einstein

(WRITE MONTH HERE)

(WRITE MONTH HERE)

(WRITE MONTH HERE)

Whoa! You're Doing great!

LIST YOUR TOP 3 *Gratitude* MOMENTS FOR THE LAST MONTH

1.

2.

3.

WHAT ARE 5 *exciting* THINGS I'D LIKE TO DO IN THE NEXT DECADE?

1. _____

_____

_____

_____

2. _____

_____

_____

_____

3. _____

_____

_____

_____

4. _____

_____

_____

_____

5. _____

_____

_____

_____

Life is not measured by the number of *breaths* we take, but by the *moments* that take our breath away.

—MAYA ANGELOU

YOU'VE NOW REACHED A MILESTONE!
YOU ARE 6 MONTHS INTO THIS *gratitude* JOURNEY

RECORD YOUR TOP 3 GRATITUDE MOMENTS FROM THE LAST 3 MONTHS
(THAT'S ONE FOR EACH MONTH)
YOU CAN DO IT!

1. _____

2. _____

3. _____

HOW TO DRAW A rainbow

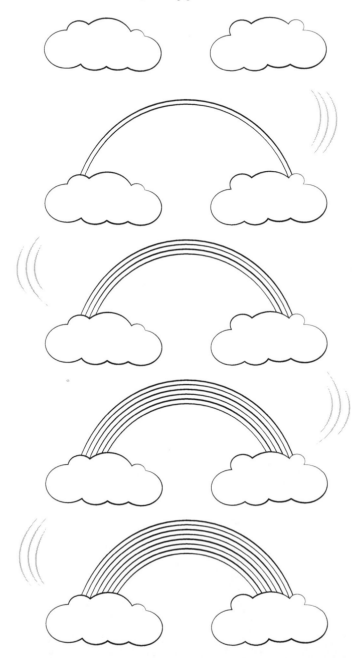

NOW YOU TRY!

GETTING TO KNOW *me*!

THINGS I LIKE AT THIS STAGE OF MY LIFE:

- 1. _____

- 2. _____

- 3. _____

SEE, THAT WAS EASY, RIGHT?

"Now this is the *confidence* that we have in Him, that if we ask anything according to His will, He *hears* us."

—1 John 5:14

(WRITE MONTH HERE)

(WRITE MONTH HERE)

(WRITE MONTH HERE)

LIST YOUR TOP 3 *Gratitude* MOMENTS FOR THE LAST MONTH

- 1
- 2
- 3

No matter how *wonderful* things used to be, we cannot *live* in the past. The *joy* and *excitement* we feel here and now are more important.

—Marie Kondo

(WRITE MONTH HERE)

(WRITE MONTH HERE)

(WRITE MONTH HERE)

LIST YOUR TOP 3 *Gratitude* MOMENTS FOR THE LAST MONTH

- 1 _____

- 2 _____

- 3 _____

"I KNOW THE *plans* I HAVE FOR YOU," SAYS THE *Lord*. "THEY ARE PLANS FOR *good* AND NOT FOR DISASTER, TO GIVE YOU A *future* AND A *hope*.

—JEREMIAH 29:11

(WRITE MONTH HERE)

(WRITE MONTH HERE)

(WRITE MONTH HERE)

LIST YOUR TOP 3 *Gratitude* MOMENTS FOR THE LAST MONTH

- 1
- 2
- 3

PRACTICE *grace* & *encouragement*
BY WRITING A LETTER TO MYSELF ON MY WORST DAY EVER.

Spend time with *God*.
Do one kind *thing*.
Shut the screens off. Be all in.
Take *care* of myself.

—T.J. Mousetis

YOU'VE NOW REACHED A MILESTONE!
YOU ARE 9 MONTHS INTO THIS *gratitude* JOURNEY

RECORD YOUR TOP 3 GRATITUDE MOMENTS FROM THE LAST 3 MONTHS.
(THAT'S ONE FOR EACH MONTH)
YOU CAN DO IT!

1. _____
_____
_____
_____

2. _____
_____
_____
_____

3. _____
_____
_____
_____

You is *kind*.
You is *smart*.
You is *important*.

—KATHRYN STOCKETT

HOW TO DRAW A *butterfly*

NOW YOU TRY!

(WRITE MONTH HERE)

(WRITE MONTH HERE)

(WRITE MONTH HERE)

Great work!

LIST YOUR TOP 3 *Gratitude* MOMENTS FOR THE LAST MONTH

1.

2.

3.

God, grant me the *serenity* to accept the things I can not change, the *courage* to change the things that I can, and the *wisdom* to know the difference.

—Reinhold Neibuhr

(WRITE MONTH HERE)

(WRITE MONTH HERE)

(WRITE MONTH HERE)

Nice!

LIST YOUR TOP 3 *Gratitude* MOMENTS FOR THE LAST MONTH

· 1 _____
_____
_____
_____
_____

· 2 _____
_____
_____
_____
_____

· 3 _____
_____
_____
_____
_____

WHEN THINGS *feel* LIKE THEY ARE FALLING APART, THEY COULD BE *falling* INTO PLACE.

"ALL THINGS *work* TOGETHER FOR GOOD FOR THOSE WHO *love* HIM."

—ROMANS 8:28

(WRITE MONTH HERE)

(WRITE MONTH HERE)

(WRITE MONTH HERE)

LIST YOUR TOP 3 *Gratitude* MOMENTS FOR THE LAST MONTH

- 1
- 2
- 3

HOW TO DRAW A *snowflake*.

NOW YOU TRY!

COWARDS FALTER, BUT DANGER IS OFTEN *overcome* BY THOSE WHO *nobly* DARE.

—QUEEN ELIZABETH II

YOU'VE NOW REACHED A MILESTONE!
YOU ARE 12 MONTHS INTO THIS *gratitude* JOURNEY

RECORD YOUR TOP 3 GRATITUDE MOMENTS FROM THE LAST 3 MONTHS.
(THAT'S ONE FOR EACH MONTH)
YOU CAN DO IT!

1. _____

2. _____

3. _____

YOU DID IT! YAY!
YOU'VE JUST RECORDED MOMENTS OF *gratitude* FOR 12 MONTHS.

CELEBRATE! HERE YOU CAN REVIEW YOUR JOURNAL AND FIND YOUR TOP 6 MOMENTS OF *gratitude* FOR THE ENTIRE YEAR.

1.

2.

3.

4.

5.

6.

I HAVE LEARNED THAT THERE IS MORE *power* IN A GOOD *strong* HUG THAN IN A THOUSAND *meaningful* WORDS.

—ANN HOOD

(HAVE YOU HUGGED SOMEONE TODAY?)

YOU THOUGHT YOU WERE DONE,
BUT THERE'S ONE MORE THING TO DO.

FINISH THE 3RD GETTING TO KNOW *me*!

THINGS I LIKE AT THIS STAGE OF MY LIFE:

- 1 _____

- 2 _____

- 3 _____

DID YOURS CHANGE FROM THE BEGINNING OF THE BOOK?

THANKS SO MUCH TO THE FOLLOWING CONTRIBUTORS AND SUPPORTERS!

GRAPHIC DESIGN: AMELIA BOWLIN
BOWLINDZGN@GMAIL.COM

MANDALA COLORING PAGES:
WWW.ETSY.COM/SHOP/SWEETGOO

WILDFLOWER GRATITUDE COLORING PAGE:
WWW.ETSY.COM/SHOP/ARTWILDFLOWERSDIGI

THANK YOU TO TONY, WHO KEPT ASKING ME IF MY BOOK WAS DONE YET. YOUR EXTRA PUSH HELPED ME GET MY IDEAS ON PAPER. LOVE YOU!

THANKS TO MY SWEET GIRLS, ALLISON AND SARAH, WHO HAVE WAY MORE CREATIVITY THAN I HAVE EVER POSSESSED. YOU ARE A BLESSING AND YOU KEEP ME ON MY TOES!

CONNECT WITH US!
#MYLITTLEGRATITUDEJOURNAL

Made in the USA
San Bernardino, CA
28 April 2016